LARKSONG STATIC:
SELECTED POEMS 2005 -2020

Martin Malone

First published 2020 by The Hedgehog Poetry Press

Published in the UK by
The Hedgehog Poetry Press
5, Coppack House
Churchill Avenue
Clevedon
BS21 6QW

www.hedgehogpress.co.uk

ISBN: 978-1-913499-01-3

9 8 7 6 5 4 3 2 1

A CIP Catalogue record for this book is available from the British Library.

Printed by TJ Books Limited, Padstow, Cornwall.

i.m.

Bob Lewis & Gerry Breen

Contents

'Articulation is the tongue-tied's fighting.'

Tony Harrison, *On Not being Milton*

BARBURY CASTLE

Meet me at the earthworks
            in the small hours on the hill.
Up there, above your childhood,
            at the swing-door of first light
as - mouthful of stars -
            another time-laden night
does its excuse-me with the dawn.

Here, beyond the tidemark
            of Swindon's dirty ochre,
power up the heart's deep electric
            and bring to me your darkness.
Let me reach towards its livewire
            its larksong static, earth your now
in the harebells, ox eye, horseshoe vetch.

Meet me at the earthworks:
            murus gallicus, univallate,
gate-gone to cowslip, chalkhill blue,
            bolt-shot to harebell and to you.
And, to you, I too am wide open;
            under the ages' weight of starlight
and slow time; waiting for the day.

ECLOGUE

Anything from a polecat to a dryad
could be stepping from this wood
into Tuesday light but it is you,
ten years back down the Ridgeway path.
Hitching up those jeans, you reach to take
my hand, palm off doubt, knuckle faith
onto ringless fingers. This isn't you
– this feral stuff – low impulse being
more my thing but that day you push me
up against a tree as old as Silbury.
We emerge from the thicket-gloom aglow
with escape and getting away with it;
it an, as yet, indeterminate: some fuzzy
co-ordinate on a half-sketched map.

Today I stick to the downland track
that skirts the spot, though stop to look.
Anything from a polecat to a dryad
could be stepping from the wood
into this light but it was you,
among the things I could not see.

WOOD ON THE DOWNS

After Paul Nash

We have been here before. Uffington, Hackpen,
Grim's Ditch, Ogbourne St.George, Wayland's Smithy,
Sparshott Firs, Bishopstone and Barbury;
all the trodden way from Overton
to Beacon Hill. Each place its *genius loci,*
a favourite colour: Ash-Blue, Ochre,
Payne's Grey, Terra-Verte, Lamp Black, Sienna.
But today you ditch your winter tones
and bid for late spring. The trees are in leaf,
the chalk from the downland reflects light
from a milder sky. *Through field glasses
one sees a landscape that one can see
in no other way.* Here, then, is yours:
the stiff cilia of trunks – a brown-fringed
platoon lost on Hill 60 – ghosts of the vortex,
the leaching colours of pending summer,
the breast, lumbar and hip curve of hill
prone upon the bed of Buckinghamshire.
And there I join you eighty years away,
with my Trojan girl; lifting her face
to mine in the dappled light of the wood.
We have been here before.

AT UFFINGTON

You stepped back a pace to better
your gaze into the low winter sun
and frame the prospect: man bends
to boy with kite and deals with a rogue
top button – a candle flame inclined
to the draught at the door of implied
fatherhood. You too fasten this moment
smiling at its easy eternity;
its archetype of family
held safe, all the same, against
the chill of our unravelling.
I'll later drive north, the tug
of necessary space pulling
me back into normal orbit.

But, for now, we stand on Dragon Hill,
our own slain myth bleeding circumstance
onto hope. The boy persists;
circles the bare chalk patch, his arm
forty-five degrees supplicant:
Epona's child of flight and air
favoured, forsaken, lifted again.
Fertility, death and healing: chaff
for the horse goddess. The fickle line
rises. Your restive hand finds mine,
capricious in turn. Caught beyond
caution, we rejoin the moment;
driving deep the flint of it into
the chalky quick of ancient time.
Scouring out our own curt lore
under the dancing hooves of
a white horse.

RED KITES AT UFFINGTON

The hunting pair stirs
a lazy spoon of air   above the coombe.

Milvus milvus
– imminent as snow in the second before fall –
turning upon
the axis of self.
There.
A reeling this of this,
the element 'I' circling
in a plughole pull of want.

This ground is incidental,
good only for carrion
or missable
drift.

And Sunday stops its junket,
holds still awhile to watch:
red-meat method of vole,
silent drone of shrew,
leveret shock and awe.

Lear's detested daughter
– driven from Tudor parish
for the price on her carcass –
is back
above
the Berkshire Downs
and all the birds of Oxfordshire
and all the birds of Oxfordshire
and all the birds of Oxfordshire...

BEST KITE ON THE HILL

Back at Uffington, the line heavier now
with a history; its haul weighty
beyond the burden of ground hefty
with its own tales. You, me and your son
and the best kite on the hill.
Passing around the string, sharing the pull
of possibility, we are shaken;
shuddering through the kite-tail spine
of ourselves, alone in the moment's blue
latitude. I look from boy to you
with some sense of new gravities.
An inkling load guyed skyward, upon
the caught breath of an idea murmured
into your ear: you, me, us. The boy turns
away, hood hoisted against the breeze;
lost to the glider's warp: Epona's
child yet. His soul at anchor there,
dragging the pale kedge of nine year-old
shoulder, quickens at its easy primacy;
steady in the heaven of his summer.
The foregone chronicles of a million
ghosts haunt the vaulted arc of air
that drags at the bellied line. Yet, whilst
others struggle to cheat the pull of
primeval earth, the white horse favours
him with the lift of new stories;
silently mouthed to himself alone,
rapt in the kite's thrumming NOW.
Shall we not figure in these fables?
Up there, do we find our correlative?
Or, loaded with history, circumstance
and doubt, do we quiver, veer and fall?
Shot falcons, ploughing ourselves
back into the waiting hillside.

SEATON CAREW, 1979

I once was a prize bingo wage slave
marking your card for six bob an hour.
Evening stints on the mic, doing it right,

white trash m.c. toastin' rhymes, any line
or four corners. Mates said my voice was pure
Shelley but, never mind the Buzzcocks,

this was business: Kelly's eye, Maggie's den,
baker's dozen, two fat ladies, lucky seven.
When I wasn't calling or checking boards,

I was painting manky outside walls
to *Heart of Glass* from the waltzers next-door.
Soon turned out to be a pain in the ass

so I asked to have back the microphone.
To be alone in the box shelling ping-pongs
from their plastic pod; saving their random

skins from the angry swarm of compressed air.
You were living just a mile up the prom,
Mam far from happy to see me your man.

Bingo called, don't move your markers,
hands off my daughter, wait for the check.

DIGITALIS

Between his first and third heart attack
passed my father's Summer of Love.
An unknown younger man came back:

my ear-ring was no longer mocked
-nor the tattoo of an arrowed dove-
between his first and third heart attack.

A sudden awareness of hip-hop and rap
a shuffling of beat groups with dub;
as an unknown younger man came back.

I'd come across him trying on hats
and found him once weeping at foxgloves
between his first and third heart attack.

Aware that given time is not given back,
he started bending lifelong rules enough
to let me see the younger man come back.

Dad was Dylan, McCartney, Jack Kerouac
in that last fond Summer of Love;
between his first and third heart attack
when an unknown younger man came back.

DECADES

I'm driving my mother
through Connemara; on the shortest day
of the year. Lenaun, Kylemore,
Cashel, Cong, Maam Cross, Letterfrack:
the names slipping sequentially
through the gloom, a rosary
of sung syllables through the knuckled
hours. Stone field, bog, lough, rock, bay,
swan, lough, bog, bay, field, stone.
It's her seventieth birthday.
Glory be to the Father,
and to the Son and to the Holy
Spirit and to something else
I can't quite name: a memory
maybe, a nurtured reflex or ghost
of the small boy that walks me yet.
Hauling me down to Stations
or Benediction, we bonded
through the resentment of missed
Blake's Seven and mumbled decades.
My tribal drum was the rhythm
of words and words repeated;
phrases circling back upon them-
selves, like country lanes leading
to unclear crossroads. Snapping
to at the memory bell, I am summoned
to this newer communion
with the drunken crow of Ireland's roads.

It is getting late. In my rear-view
the solstice sun thins out
against the wild Atlantic as
before me, black and huge, *Croagh Patrick*
mars the horizon with the dark
obligation of an evening
Mass from a Sunday teatime long
ago. Greater still, my mother
in the passenger seat; the decades
dropping from her sleeping face
till she's the girl emerging
from *John Collier's* factory gates
into my father's embrace.
I am stumbling around
in the back seat of our clapped-out A40;
trying to get a better view, sniffing
a moment with the gusto of my
full four-and-three-quarter years.

Later, at a smart restaurant
back in Westport,
it is she who will stumble;
words eluding
her in the stress of what
she thinks expected of her. Sure
before her God, she wavers
before the cutlery. The chef's
questions demanding the response
of an unfamiliar creed.
In a gesture learnt
from her, I reach out
across the space, hand enfolding hand,
fingers guiding fingers
to the right prayer; grasp,
at last, upon the right bead.

LIVERPOOL-IRISH

My father endured the taunts of 'tick'
(from a man called Keenan) and bore
the nickname 'Paddy' uneasily;
yet would stiffen to the reel
and set his jaw for the camera.

He would laugh at the Pier Head Irish,
gazing out beyond the river's foggy mouth
to a neglectful motherland, through eyes
distant in drink and false memory;
doing his maths on the round and neatly

balancing its cost against that to re-buy
the family farm. Yet he was in clover
to hear his name in *The Irish Rover*
and talked of cousins in Wicklow
with the requisite exile's glow.

This celtic *mestizo* thing is awkward.
Fit to be called diaspora, commodified
in song, yet welcome back but slowly,
when we've stayed away too long: history's
tenant cousins twice-removed.

I was once suspect enough for passport
stamps, *MON DROIT* and my name to keep me
all day in Holyhead for routine questions
though my accent's enough still to Cromwell our pitch
in some *gaeltacht* pub in Ballynahinch.

MIC-ING THE KIT

"Here space is everything, for time ceases to quicken memory."
(Gaston Bachelard, *The Poetics of Space*.)

My favourite hour of any session was
mic-ing the kit. Beyer, Electrovoice,
Neumann, Sennhauser, AKG and Shure;
sensitive diaphragms, phantom power.

Analogue, unsampled and raw, this
the real business of capturing sound:
the cottage loaf of pressure gradients,
the sideways heart of cardioid response.

Often, I would send away the drummer,
ply him with tea or weed to leave me there
- free of his twitches and random hits -
alone with his kit, sexing it in space.

There were the routine no-brainers, holy
trinities and givens: bass drum, hi-hat
and snare meant the egg of the D-twelve,
C-four-one-four, SM fifty-seven.

There was the metalwork and toms, beloved
of drummers loathed by myself. I always
did my best by them: stringing up condensers,
top mic-ing the mounted mids, crash and ride.

Then things got interesting in the room
with your own little signatures or tricks.
A woodcutter now, you knew the grain
of the space; its sweet spots and hard-knots.

The snare's true *logos* was to be had reflected
from some wall or favourite corner; it's kingfisher
reverb caught fire in a Gents' urinal,
where the porcelain gave sympathetic decay.

Making my way back to the control room
through the vineyard of leads, through the heavy
anechoic doors, I was usually happy.
Artisan's work: preparing the dance.

HAAS EFFECT

For John Martyn

Between 30 and 40 milliseconds,
the human ear incorporates sounds
arriving from two separate sources;
letting time drift beyond that duration
before perceiving them as distinct:
that's as *delay* (audio effect) or,
in common terms, *echo* (phenomenon).
Observing this law of the first wave front
is an involuntary sensory inhibition
mirrored in your memory;
the acoustics of which can be cruel.

So, a new amputee is tortured by
the invisible itch and reaches down
to scratch solid air, before advancing
toward his future on unsteady leg.
And I am awake before dawn, hearing
a voice and embracing space, with you
already two hours away; effecting
your own precedence in some fast lane,
to a motorway's flattened grey wave
of white noise and forgetting...

WAITING FOR THE *GREEN* WORLD TOUR TO COME TO TOWN

Late morning slinks its way into the attic flat;
dances dust motes over gin-bottles and underwear;
takes its place at my shoulder to laser the scene.
You're both yet asleep in our impossible single bed,
it's May '89 and these those final weeks of the sense
of possibility that has graced our mid-Twenties.
Lo shifts in her rest, woozily coming-to while you
drool like the cat when happy and sat in her lap.
I steal into the kitchen, make coffee quietly,
drape a towel over my arm, and bring through breakfast –
your comedy butler in a vest and pair of stray knickers.
We're waiting for the *Green* World Tour to come to town,
absurdly wired and alive to the crazed eloquence
of each other's obsession; high on what we'll learn
to be 'dopamine', though we need no such explanation.
What we want is the gig and Buck's guitar, Michael's
psycho dancing, Berry's eyebrows, Mikey's specs.
We want what we've already got but do not yet know:
a perfect circle of acquaintances and friends. Sex
is something else, the chorus to our bigger song,
love is the handwritten thirty-page letter kept this long.
I just wanted to tell you, just wanted you to know.

LIKE I WAS YOUR GIRLFRIEND

Afterwards, I step out into the yard,
shaking the silver from your jumper,
the punkish one I bought when last home.

And now we've completed the look:
you are John Lydon, a young Strummer,
you are your son, the spit of me.

When you put your glasses on, we are
both your grandfather, Bobby, shorn
back to life by my ham-fisted razor.

Handing you your wig, I try on heartache
for size but it no more fits this evening than
the day when, aged four, I wore your hat.

We laugh at your new cut – it takes years
off you – but most of all we are relieved
that you carry it off, deep in your bones.

LORDS OF THE RING

Now that was a world order Aunt Norah
could understand: fat lads and uncles tucked
into spandex, proving nimble with Saturdays.
While East and West faced off, the big boys
got to grips in some grunting town hall.

Warrenpoint and moonwalks were nothing to her,
so long as Dickie Davies rolled up
with his *Mallen* streak and kipper tie;
glint in his eye and tache well-groomed.
He can light up any room, that lad, said
she on her knees beside the grate.

Giant Haystacks got her riled when, behind
the referee's back, he leathered Leon Arras
the Man from Paris, though that was nothing
to her scorn for Harvey Smith or the way
Pat Roach knocked out The Nature Boy.

While '77 was The Pistols and Jubilee,
for me it was the sight of Norah
tearing raw meat from the telly as
Big Daddy unmasked Kendo Nagasaki:
Do him Shirley! He's a nasty bugger!

What she liked was how Les Kellett always
seemed out-on-his-feet but managed to win,
the way Catweazle tickled Mick McManus
into submission and a distant sadness
in the lost blue eyes of Jackie Pallo.

THAT WINTER

After a month of snow came the rains:
chugging against the tide up Meaburn Edge,
peering through mizzle towards High Cup Nick,
all-but-stalling in lakes on the Reagill road.

The martins' nest grew sodden and heavy;
broke its spittle moorings after the night
of gales, played mud-pies with my bedroom sill
then feasted on the garden table.

Mornings were night-black and blue with cold:
big icicles snottered the gable end,
drive time was lost scraping rime off the car,
while great tits diminished in the hard frost.

The Lyvennet heron, a leggy grey clock,
met me at the gate each day; his fish round,
pulling in at the rock below the weir,
let me know if I was early or late.

Past October, the neighbours went part-time,
became a T.V.'s blue glow, chimney smoke
or *Berghaus* dummy: muffling good mornings
through zipped-up layers of Gore-Tex and wool.

The weir's white noise was my rock n' roll;
rose and fell with the flow and one night
coughed up a tree that stuck to its palate
for seven weeks, changing my lullaby

that winter, that bloody winter.

WHAT THOUGHT DID

Undivides black from its star,
dissolves salt from days
which mourn that space lost
between ourselves and sleep
this morning in the forest,
as you wash your hair
in a mountain stream,
the blue smoke
rising from our fire
to parse wild taints of berry
from our tongues,
while everything is ours
or was or shall or may be
every night, every leaf, every loss.

MAP-MAKING

You live close to this land,
map its contours as surely
as your body's own:
secret parting of valley lips,
arterial push of river into tide,
the sticky rill of your own still water.

Some days you plot another's country,
their muscle and bone becoming yours
in the close-ribbed cabin
that domiciles a heart.
And always, after dark,
you strip his night to its secret,
claim the ground as your estate
before bringing yourself to a trust,
that never quite comes.

Here, inscribe my shoulder's span
while I etch the gravity of your waist,
each ink as black as the other's,
the survey essential to both.
Cartographers then,
let us share our dismal craft.
We live close to this land,
unmap its contours as surely
as our own: its occult
debris and dead ends.

THE INTERPRETER'S HOUSE

"If Blake could do this when he rose up from shite
What might he not do if he sat down to write."
(William Blake, *'When Klopstock England defied'*, 1800)

With bread at sixpence a quartern, it is better
to work in the country than starve in a city,
so the Interpreter packs for the coast:

sixteen boxes from Lambeth to Sussex,
copper plate, burins, furniture and ink;
her handmade clothes, his wooden press.

Not much to show for the company of Angels,
no flash portmanteau on the road to Zion,
But here the wind sweeps through the cornfield

with the clamour of souls, gales sigh in the thatch
and the shifting light of his first-viewed sea forms
the shape of a man particle-bright with Eternity.

Here, there is purple thyme, clematis above
the gate and an elm overlooking the Downs;
here, birdsong and odours of the happy ground.

September, and it starts well enough:
The Bread of sweet Thought & the Wine of Delight
Feeds the Village of Felpham by day & by night.

He learns Latin and Greek, takes on Hebrew
that he may speak to God in his own tongue,
notes how meat is cheaper than in London.

Los descends daily and from him the sea
trawls visions of Albion; shoals Cherubim
in quicksilver glints of how it might be.

Then winter's damp climbs through cellar-less floors,
Fever & Toil – the poor man's *aqua fortis* – corrode
his Golden Net and hell is Hayley's commission.

Jerusalem so begins but remains unbuilt,
the sword stays awake in yellowing hands
and a downland cottage comes up to let
in England's green & pleasant Land.

MUSANDAM

Musandam this Spring, and it catches me
unawares: you below the waterline, striped
with sunlight, shade and a sudden renewal;
the tidal come and go of your limbs
to the elver rhythm of the first stroke
taught you by your daddy when you were five.
Your legs forcep buoyancy from the waters
of *Khor Ash Sham* as I fill my lungs and dive
once more down to the point of salvage:
this coralline shard of your living moment,
its passing prefigured in the pallor
of your sunken skin, its quickening a flux
of dark anemone upon the pubic bone.
Head above water, all is every day:
you smiling back at me and our good luck,
the *bedu* bond of salt yet in our guts
to cover the three days here and those three
beyond. It is back down there that everything
is reconceived and passion recommenced.
Through the memory-milt of gulf water
I am brought up short and see
anew the dhow-curve of your middle;
the pelvis set back, like an African girl's,
the buttocks high and compact. Your circling
arms conduct an elegant stop-frame switch
of direction, clear of the island reef.
I surface again and take in the vista:
Musandam's broken fist of limestone
shaken forever at Persia. This was
a pearl coast. Exfoliate but fifty years
from the oil-greased palm of Arabia
and you have the calloused hands
of oarsmen, pulling out to the beds to plunge
long and deep beyond the mortal breath
into zones such as this; redeeming
iridescence from the oyster dark.

With this as my blade, I dive once more
to prise the unworded hinge of moments
such as these: you below the waterline,
in concrete time, reflecting your own light.

CAFÉ CASTIGNOLLES

Things quietened down after Tony left town,
in his wake a grudge and way too much love
to keep him safe in the lifestyle he'd known.

Seba sold his share in the bar soon after,
re-trained as a sea captain, ran aground
and, in two wild years, blew the goddam lot.

Then Paps quit to open his own place, just
around the corner. It's good, his daughter
cooks with him and us they well remember.

Maité grew wings after that tough winter,
escaped town with a younger guy to open
a flower shop but still keeps in touch.

Fabiénne and Mark went their separate ways,
he with his crazy *chica,* she with a local lad
who was bonny and rich and gave her a son.

Then, of course, the deaths: Louis and Gina both,
shy Maurice, whose blue eyes you made shine,
Thiérry's wife and Didier the *véloist.*

This old place you would barely recognize:
the walls, the doors, the floors, all changed
except for the bed, that bloody great bed.

24 RUE CARNOT

This house lolls in a droiling back street.
The army-issue blanket of working week sleep
is rolled aside for a thousand-egg omelette
that duvets dreams of fish and strange meetings.

In this bed I drive to Lagrasse to chat
to a long dead friend in some doorway;
him blue-eyed and smiling, while the mistral
shifts the dust around our cat-shod toes.

The early bells of St. Maurice tickle slumber
in the slow flow of morning hours, tease
my waking with the hyper-real as a stream
of lost lovers skim light across my belly.

That *Velux* rasp of rain on roof-window
lowers the room's lid and drives me back to this:
a child's rest again, our tangle of limbs,
these dreams and, on a clear night, your star.

TRUMAN ON ISCHIA

The room chooses itself: a writer's space
with a balcony above the harbour,
two chairs, table and a tortured old bed.
Its provenance comes later, as she pours
us Lachrimae Christi and talk turns
to the *buena séra* under a sky of early stars.

I forget why we came here - your sister
perhaps - but here are we in Forio
on Boxing Day in Capote's old room
at the *Pensione de Lustro*; both town
and coincidence as intimate
and satisfying as one's own heartbeat.

Islands are like ships at permanent anchor,
no place for the rush of hours; the dropped watch
an outrageous bit of symbolism to prove
his point. Crossing the tiles, I see Truman
on the balcony as the Virgin comes to town;
forgetting to throw his votive ribbons.

In forty-nine, Signora Mussolini still sat
out her quiet exile in shabby black
and the town's two idiots claimed their island
in the afternoon's white midnight.
Maria watered her drinks, Gioconda awaited
a letter and her spring was the longest ever.

The longest and the loveliest.

PIAZZA

After Giacometti

Seven AM in *Piazza Plebescito,*
not the human figure but long shadows
cast in this bronze light of April morning.
Freeze the frame. Bookshop owner opening
up on *Piazza Dante,* the Crib Street
assistant with her new lover to meet,
a Mergellina fisherman dropping
off fresh vongole, the Vomero lawyer
and Caremar sailor bound for Ischia:
ghosts of the unreal city, thin as nails.

He'd make your head look like the blade of a knife.

MONT SAINTE-VICTOIRE

Cézanne as Sisyphus: each day climbing
the steep sides of self, a mountain on his back,

to lose the light, to not quite get right the it,
the it-of-it. Rolling back down him each night

towards the morning; a mountain on his back,
each day climbing: Cézanne as Sisyphus.

GHOST OF A GENIUS

"First of all the art of living", PAUL KLEE

Black smudges
where his hand
rested
on the paper
give it away:
stitches of moment,
breath-frosted glass.

All genius
is puppetry.
Time, disease and early death
– the string-pulling fingers –
dance duration
down a path to eternity.

Take away the ghost
and you have what it is.
Large eyes, cropped beard,
the tilted, domed head,
arms flopping down
under the weight of fatherhood:
a toy for Felix Paul.

His masterpiece.

HOUSE BY THE RAILROAD

It was all about parallels, that house
on Ocean Road: running lines laddering
the level gust of coastal track,
those vertical shafts of Doric column,
the long tracking shot of its upstairs lounge
that held on the North Sea's horizon.
And that little life with mine; waving back
at me from the attic room which never
opened, as I crossed the bridge to the Dene;
from there to the shore and on out to sea.

ARCHIVES

After Christian Boltanski

We are all so complicated,
                                        then die;
from one stage pass quickly
to the next, become
          objects that were someone.

The eye seeks out pattern and is satisfied.
What can you see
          in a darkened room:
ten columns of three,
saints' bones for the century?

Each one has his own life,
                              each her own story:
the children of Dijon,
          unknown person,
stolen graduates of Vienna.

Into every eye shines a light,
          its wires trailing clumsily
down the wall,
and beneath each face,
          a tin box for the soul.

CUR

A tipping point of sorts;
dress it as watershed, crossroads or crest
but we hurl ourselves

downhill

into the fuck of it:
arse over tit,
cock, mouth and clicket.

That point which snuffs out tenderness
with need – ragged and drooling – stinks out
the den with sweat, juice and focus.

In the coop we take more than we need,
delight in the ease of our carnage,
so do with me.

The pack is hard by,
famished with intent.

PRODIGALS

Friday Night: 9:30

The cancelled train of last week's lost high
now behind us, we ease deep into chairs,
each snugging the glove of shared hunger.
Our deferred pleasure in escape declares
itself open for business with a glass
of good wine and the glance that reads
my returning gaze. We let minutes pass
this way, just us looking, here in Leeds
in a hotel with its booked double room.

Then have to laugh and for no real reason, how
people do who've been long-parted. How it is
sometimes, when you finally make it home.
So, let us bring home the gift of days. Now
teach me exile, show me lost hearths.

Friday Night 10:30: Your Jonathans/My Helens

Yes, we will honour them but the nature
of this beast is a here-and-now: the only
thing we've an interest in. Now, as your tongue
meets mine in a slow uncoiling of other.
Now, as my mouth finds your neck,
and the wolf paws hard at the door.
Now as I hold you here in the NOW of us.
Let the record show that there are no records:
Alexandria is burning, our small histories gone
in a welter of lost wonders and cancelled account.
Indeed, we will honour them but they *shall*
step aside. Then onto this table, that sofa,
into an empty lift: our own snatched rosary
until, finally, we make it to a bed.

Saturday Morning: 7AM

Sunlight solders the morning into place
mote-by-mote, lasered almost to portrait:

you as *Still Life*, you as *Reclining Nude*.
Yes, let us play this game and go there,

trace the stages and versions that led us
to now and this man watching you sleep.

Armed only with guesswork, he stands
in the early light, drawing together

some sense of a life before you met;
sketching outline and general form,

exercising the privilege of transposition:
one year moved to the next, connectedness

given to isolated stones, lone trees granted
hillsides. Inkling shades of the unknown.

Sunday Morning: 10AM

Saturday night wakes up on the bathroom scales;
weighs out its carnage in mermaids' tails,
bra, lube, seraphim, the keys to a stolen car.
Blinking, we survey this Sunday church bazaar;
wondering what to do with it all now,
knowing we will buy the lot anyhow.
We pay over the odds for something gone so fast,
hand over hard cash to save this from the past,
making up for our sense of lost time:
our darndest struggle to make all this rhyme.

Outside our hotel room what passes for a spire
lifts from a neighbouring church, the day tires
before 10AM and we go back to bed secure
in what we know will last, what we hope endures.

Monday Morning: 8:30 AM

And all there was between them then was rain.
And all there is between us now, this train
and my copy of *The Mersey Beat,* lying spent
across the guilty pleasure of your novel.
Our legs touch beneath the table, still caught
in the mad-mangled crocodile of the past
forty-eight hours. We chaperone the space
above, make Monday love in the negative.

Next stop is yours and we're cutting it fine
for that connection. You know what, let's not.
Let's not make it; neither yours nor mine. Just
turn around and do it all again and keep on
doing it until we change weeks, months, years
into this weekend. We can do that, right?

ALICE

I give you this, my snow-and-blackthorn heartland
and its morning heron in the beck,
my Viking Lyvennet with its boltwood bridge.

Water pools darkly on the weir's brow,
down the fish-bridge chicanes
a rill, subtle as lamprey.

Fanged with ice, the bank's mossy walrus
talks to me of many things: our last-nights
and mornings, your dawn-lit flesh and sleep.

Sleep on while I bend to pluck these stems:
cold ivory from which to carve a chess set,
frore gimlets with which to plant a kiss.

Then you're beside me, in a wind-tumbled
fluster of rooks and their cracked peppercorn
of song. My gift you take upon your lips,

kiss fingers back to life,
tease summer from the ice.

SMALL LIGHTNINGS

Driving the A4 to Burghclere, last summer
passes me in an ambulance

on the opposite side. The flashing lights
tell me all I need to know: our time

here is taking its leave on a gurney;
worked at by paramedics whose

urgency is slipping with each
failed shock. I do as Dave says

and stand clear. In doing so I see
she looks very much like you

as you slept through your fever,
those three December days in my room.

When you finally came to, you smiled
and pulled me on top of you. Though now,

it's not looking so good for last summer.
I glimpse your tattoo on her shoulder

as he bends over to massage
the pale ribcage. This year

there is no give-back of lightning.
Dave I say, *we're losing her.*

SUNDERING

There are no rules but your own
and these are open to negotiation.

Not thinking helps but is, rather,
in the spirit of the game than a rule as such.

Not looking is both advisable and covered
by rules 1a through to 3c. High-speed

internet access and misuse of social media
are strongly discouraged (*see: Rule Nine*).

Under the laws of the game, that which was close
flips to the wrong end of your telescope.

Each dawn sees you bury the corpse
only to dig it up again at midnight; this

is purely at the discretion of the arbiter.
One of the players will walk away without looking back,

carrying their grief, like St. Christopher, to the other side.
The other will stumble from one memory to another,

blinding themself in the sharp light of flashback.
Whilst this is not legislated for, it is permitted

under the general code of participant conduct.
What you must understand is that

the rules are not here to ensure fair play,
but a way out of this mess.

ON AN AFTERNOON LIKE THIS SHE TAKES A NEW LOVER

This afternoon you meet your new lover.
I'm in the outfield waiting on catches
while you smile and give back his gaze.
I bend to dry my palms in the June dust
as you raise your glass beside a canal.
I cross to the other side of the square.
You note that he is left-handed, like me.
As you sidestep the man-trap of memory,
I revive an old Scott Walker song.

A wagtail threads its flight-path left to right
in the seconds his hand lingers on your leg.
And as you watch him walk into the pub
you make your decision, while measuring
his length for the cabin bed. In my head
you are nowhere as the ball arcs skyward
and swirls my way. Steadying ourselves,
we prepare for the afternoon's moment.
This says I will drop it. This says he will fit.

MRS. MOUNTER CIRCA.1914

You have seen them come and go: the salesmen,
stevedores, undergraduates and tinkers,
lorn veterans of Omdurman and Colenso,
the struggling artist with his curious hours;
all passing through the widow's breach of spare
room. Your years lived impasto – caked-on,
palpable as Sunday Best – are rendered boldly,
dealing only in certainty, creed and nation,
dealing solidly in bricks and mortar
and the definite vertical of the doorway
that frames you as you sit, impassive
as the teapot, immovable as the rent.
Outside the world turns to mud, feeds its sons
to fire and lead and the names
you will hear for the first time:
Passchendaele, Somme, Ypres, Mons....

SEANCE

Date yourself 2014 and come;
by now it is only language
and low opportunity
calling witness
to provide
the necessary
authenticating element:
a scrawled
utter of utterness,
trench honesties
occluded by one century
and the paradigms of myth.

Even then, you had to lie.
With the advantage
of immediacy,
small wonder
the shires were sad,
small wonder
the corpse-constructed line
found its pitiful page.
What they said of it
became what it is,
though the terms to describe
do not exist.

So come,
let us sit and reconstruct;
the glass on the table
historian enough
to catch their words
and stop this rain,
to stop this rain,
to stop this rain.

LET US SLEEP NOW

Vienna, 31/7/2014

Then you spot him after all these years,
on the U3 platform at the *Westbahnhof*
heading out towards Simmering.

You glimpse his profile in the tunnel's gloom
but can't quite root that lean face,
clean and good-looking and well again.

The long summer heatwave's been good to him,
tanning his skin caramel and free
of the pallor of your last strange meeting.

A tattooed bicep strains impressively
at the t-shirt, a booted calf flexes
and there he stands in his animal prime.

You smile with recognition, catch his eye;
not Saxon or Prussian or Pomeranian
just an Austrian boy heading west again,
not your way but up the line to Simmering.

TRENCH REQUISITES

In my old soldier manner, I told him he'd soon
change his style, but he'd shrug and not listen.
So we share out the hamper left behind,

while another makes good his transition
from man to riven thing. On our minds,
the memory of a Christmas that waxed forever

over eighteen months of deadlock and shellfire,
as King & Country turns to *Quand sera-ce fini?*
and Intha Pink, once in-the-line, is growing old.

Yes, how we hate you, you cheerful young men
with your tinned kippers and today's *Daily Mail*;
the periscope from Harrods, the warm new boots;

galoshes bought yesterday in Knightsbridge;
your wire-cutters and quail eggs from Aunt Grace,
and Father's gift of an Aquascutum.

You'll get used to the smell of blood and rum,
soon learn to see, beyond the metaphors of dawn,
the blue smoke from his bacon frying and know,

here at the suicide of nations, not to chance a look.
Learn fast and perhaps you might live to out-ghost
the silence of your name hallooed twice at roll call.

NEVERENDIANS

From half-term Indians to hard-nosed veterans
in the space of a year, underage and over here,

we hunker down beneath a ridge lousy with Fritz
and know in our bones it's the war that wins wars,

that blood alone moves the wheels of history and that
this trench system, set end-to-end, might circle what

we like to call God's Earth, His good work spoiled
by the hand of man which, having written, moves on

in a scrawl of broken men but again finds time,
when out of the line at the end of a bloody day,

to slump into a dug-out, once more take up its pen
and wearily address the hopeless task of this:

It is my sorrowful duty to write to you of the death
of your son...

MR. WILLETT'S SUMMERTIME

An Act to provide for the Time in Great Britain and Ireland being in advance of Greenwich and Dublin mean time respectively in the summer months. Date of Royal Assent: 17th May 1916.

Where to begin with time? Rise early, saddle a horse and ride
out to Petts Wood. The morning, incandescent with summer,

is running over itself to get at it and it and it and daylight
is everywhere wasted on sleepers beyond drawn down blinds.

It's for toil and lovers you would save this, though the times
beat you to it, grab the minutes for coal and zero-hours

that fuel a different summer. Now we've time to die
over and over before our letters reach home

and afterwards doesn't always come behind before,
if at all. So the barman calls 'Time!', the whistle sounds

and, after synchronising our watches, we move off
around the point you notice that loosening cough.

1916, and, like many a medal, your moment arrives
post-mortem, the blinds still drawn in Petts Wood.

WANTON BOYS

After Cecil Lewis

Seventeen is not a grateful age
but they'll take you young, over-
look your lies for a roaring engine.

So you swap these carefree years
for the feer sky's new testament
of *nacelle, Pitôt, ailerons, magneto...*

A dream, conjecturable as heaven,
flight's still fresh miracle paints
its brilliance across your days,

and earth grows suddenly remote
while cirrus turns copper, fades pink
then drifts away grey into night.

Thiepval, down past Boiselle, round
the Fricourt salient and on to Mountauban,
the earth taking moonlight like moleskin,

then home to dinner and the empty chair
of a boy you'd laughed with over lunch,
lost at two thousand feet where he worked

the arc of our own guns. Summer weather
brings days of blue and crystal, heat bumps
throwing us up above the haze to circle

like flies in an August room, the air
our element over the guns continual
scintillation. From here the land

is shorn of its contours and the PBI
but dun figures labouring under kit
while we move like spirits in an airy loom.

Always in your blind spot, it is chance
we fear most: aberration, tailspin,
fire or the unforeseen.

You die alone in the clouds
and death, like the sun, is a thing
you cannot gaze on too long.

BIDDEN

after Mary Bordern

Here are cotton things
and rubber things;
here, liquids and pots.
Here are steel things
and pillows; tin boxes,
needles and glass.
Here, are labels and little
white squares of gauze.

Yes, I know
that you understand these things
but it doesn't do to think.

You pile blankets
onto his wasted body;
fetch jugs of hot water;
boil long rubber tubes
in wretched saucepans.

Their courtesy as they die,
reluctant to cause me trouble
or put me out, as I gauge
how fast a life is ebbing.

Some hurry,
chasing a last omnibus,
for others, there is no such rush,
as if savouring the slow throes
of their own obliteration.

His brain comes off in my hands
as I lift away the bandage,
Death annoyed at my fussing.

I know you understand,
but what have you
and all these things
to do with the dying
of this man?

Nothing.
Take them away.
Release has entered the room
and a miracle draws near.

RIPON WORK

They are dying again at Beaumont Hamel
as you stroll Borage Lane,
three days after your twenty-fifth birthday,
mind yet cobbled with skulls of the lads you left behind.

Spring is pushing back through the hedgerow
with lesser celandines

and along the banks of the Skell,
a kingfisher's lyddite triggers
that ghost of a twitch.

At number seven, you unlatch the gate,
take out a key and stroll up to the white front door.

Searching for peace, you retreat to the attic with its tiny skylight,
the shrieks of children playing soldiers down on the street.

Here you are Chatterton and Keats,
half in love with death's idea
while making best use of its dutiful shadow.

You write your mother, go over old drafts,
'defectuousities', and 'the inwardness of war'.

Briefly, you pause to listen to swallows *skirruping* their early return,

then back to your notes, strike-throughs,
séance and retrospection,
another time-strafed Edwardian
caught out in the open with defective kit.

The town's darkening lanes are kind to you,
gift you a send-off
and, here, sensing how it all will end,
you teach yourself to carry your cross.

NOTE: *On March 21st 1918, in the same week that Wilfred Owen turned twenty-five and rented a room in a cottage on Borage Lane, the Germans began their huge Spring offensive. Whilst in Ripon, between 12th March and June 5th, he worked on a number of his best-known poems and roughed out his Preface.*

From THE UNRETURNING

Kitchener's meme

And so it lives on long after your genes have dissolved into the deep beyond Marwick Head: Edwardian adversative, Junker's bane, stern patriarch of the call-to-arms. Shouldering past Omdurman, burying blame for that dearth of shells, your immortal soul is now a Field Marshal's cap, thousand-yard stare and the waxed moustache. Leete's icon points the way to manhood, Thiepval and a field-won name. Answering the want, see how they came, a volunteer army raised on hoardings, omnibus, tramcars and shame: off whistling for their shilling along the track of your gaze. It is still considered masterful. They have still not returned.

Flash Mob

Assembled of a sudden, we watch them go in the name of a hobby or the honour of their school, to the credit of their trade, for the roots of a name, for the streets of their town, for the *kudos* of the game: Tyneside Irish, London Welsh, Arts & Crafts, West Belfast, Stockbrokers, City, Public Schools, Bicycles, Football, Battersea, Hull, Bankers, Bristol, Bradford, Leeds, Sheffield, Rhondda, Salford Pioneers, shoulder-to-shoulder the Empire League, it's yeoman-and-yeoman and King's Own Bowmen for Brave Little Belgium and on into Berlin; the ten-street armies mustered by their masters are here because they're here, because they're here because...

Truces

So many since the war to end all need of them, but nice that our own abides to offload groceries one hundred years on. The handshake, the chocolate bars, swapped baccy and badges – those jumpers for goalposts – all snug in the myth kitty divvied up for Christmas by this flawlessly whiskered troupe. Here, no rats feast on body parts, depiction is fictional, though achingly done, and everything's based on historical fact. How shall we now witness those others from wars that didn't happen: the unremarked ceasefires of Dhofar, Derry, Sierra Leone; those gables, rough diamonds and dead *adoo* propped up as warnings in the souk at Salalah?

Clickbait

Each evening the real work starts, not at the front but in front of it: repair the wire, recover his guts, dig that sap, patrol or raid. The detail shivers in its crump-hole, funked by a Verey's glow and the unreality of it all, its goal a cornered *Hun* to bring back alive with his terror and those photographs of home. The land itself has never been so intimately known, as you snout an earth flayed of its skin. This night gets lost to all whereabouts and a dawn that lifts too quickly at your shoulder. Reduced from subaltern to silhouette, an eye narrows on the cross-hairs, somewhere on high a lark sings and off clicks the safety-catch.

Futureproof

How are we to sweat our assets now the lads are sapped to bone and Belgian humus, their death-augmented realities green-screened onto memory's shonky IMAX? Ever tricky, post-production's farmed out to global partners, where Tommy's pixelated soul recurs as *Warfare 2.1™* from the bods in Shenzhen: new features, new characters, pathos & chronotope, a shared heritage with the unseen. True to the land that bore them, the Surreys play this game as, under the field gun's brazen frenzy, the shires win their name. If love could have saved us we would not have died but die we did for all the love, post-human each, lousy with it, reeking. Please remember that you ought to remember but not like this, sweet Jesus, not like this.

Notre Dame des Brebières

Legacies of the War to Construe All Wars: my mother in *no need of surgeons*; the hunched old woman bent into an Atlantic gale, looming out of the Connemara rain that time; my own knackered hips; me urging your pram through a hail of blossom this Spring on Miller's Lane. A national diet of wistful glory and time out of joint, no story more crooked than this, the Leaning Virgin above a town square; gilded with myth, burdened with meanings that tilt it past the horizontal. As if the random shell-damage cannot be left to lie, as if some outcome depends upon a third-rate miracle. Just press 'download' and Photoshop™ them all back to vertical.

Context Collapse

Re-fried over-easy, we're consumed as ready simile: the hardcore classic of a sopping Glastonbury, the mud-brimmed Hunters of some washed-out Latitude. Of course, your "*like the bloody Somme*" is nothing of the sort and it's not us you mean. That's Third Ypres with its limitless mud bound within the nutshell of a bullet, collapsing all context into the pulp of a pal's sniped brain. There was no bad dope or robbing Scousers, no lost mobiles or broken portaloos; though we too pissed where we could and the lines, for sure, went down. For us and one unplugged minute, there was sunshine, a cigarette and in that sunken lane, the same brief brotherhood of man.

Webbing

Buy it now for two-seven-five, condition as shown in photo, too well-made to be repro, the kosher stuff of a lost patrol. As metaphors got real and euphemism ugly, the Aldershot Design lugged its rough rigging onto the dog-tired shoulders of our line. And, if you're browsing for archetype, for "how it really was", then scroll no further than this, one belt; two braces; bayonet frog; pouches for ammo; one haversack; valise with two straps and carriers for the head and helve of an E-tool. This was our hyperlink, a one-piece jacket for the universal soldier: Dai's Greatcoat, Hotspur's mail, John Ball's frayed thread for the fucked-up Grail of Mametz Wood. Epic failure/ epic fail.

Legacies

Christmas Past is Christmas Present, strolls Mesopotamia mobile in hand, buffering the orange bundle of a man beyond meaning. So at Kut we stick it out with the Poonas, waiting on the RFC's hand-dropped payload; tight in the hair's breadth between whizz-bang and telegram. The text-speak of a Field Service Postcard says enough: *we dnt cm in2 yr cts as conkrez or nmes but libr8rs.* Though, if needs be, we'll be back in black with a South London twang, in biplane or bomb-vest, to stroll into markets or drop in on uncivilized tribes. Repeat then, repeat: *Kill them all. God will know His own.* Each man blessed with just enough afterlife to teach him they were wrong.

School Run

If you've a minute, tweet this: the car-struck badger you've driven past these last two weeks, *pikelhaube* snout irate in death, body bloating with fetid air, hind-legs rigid in surrender. *Kamerad*, emptied of essence, this is the boy from your home village; that snotty kid with a terrier whose Dad liked a drink, the one who pissed himself when Miss Manning caught him with a rat in his desk. Him: always the last to put up his hand, always unlucky in love. His losing streak continued over here and now that's him rotting away to your left, hung on the brambles of a B-road: a passing stain in no man's land, fuel for the coming spring. He'll walk no more on Cotswold.

Aristeia

On CCT, I see him stab and stab again a well-killed kid from the next estate: little warrior, cock of the walk. Subaltern of the seventeen streets and their respawn army; his boys held this patch, his boys hold it still: from the Met, from the blacks from the *who-you-fucking-looking-at?* The trench is well-established as, there beyond the bypass, attrition starts where the sun goes down and the gates begin. His family has been informed and somewhere a comedian is perfecting the voice: *you is, like, dead meat innit, Blood?* Remember, if you missed the show you can catch up online, though we must warn you the following contains scenes you may find disturbing.

Combat Gnostic

In the end, you'll know little more than those *poilus* baa'ing up the line at the Aisne. All you have on them is history's widescreen, and selected ironies of hindsight – Churchill's cock-up in the Dardenelles, Benito's brush with death, Gutmann's citation and the German "field rabbinate". And, while we may now know the true cost of a Jewish Iron Cross or why the bells ring for Armistice as the telegram boy leans his bicycle against the gate, this is all we know. Uncle Alf wasn't telling, that's for sure, his gnosis wrapping stillness about the 6-year old boy who jangles Pip, Squeak & Wilfred in a room that smells of baccy, piss and Black Bullets: keys to a door he'll never open.

NOSTOS

To each hamlet a homecoming
and the ghost story it brings.
This, a slow train hauling back
the nightmare of Verdun
on his still muddy boots.
Unexpected as May frost,
step heavy under the weight
of all he's seen since leaving
the farm to a young wife,
he stops off for cognac
in a neighbourhood bar,
where few recognize
the war-altered face.
Ariége boy, home on leave,
do you pause on the track
to *Le Quié*, breath again
that ripe air of the hill's acres,
gorge on estranged silence
then stiffen to the breeze
which leads you back to her?
I see you now in the wood
above *Jacquet*, in a moment
closer than thought to one
raised in the shade of its pines.
You turn for home, hitching
your weariness onto shoulders
robbed of love, these final steps
to take you out of hell.
Poilu, they will kill you,
for what you do
to what you find
upon that bed.
They will track you down
and shoot you
for running.

In Greek epic poetry, the 'nostos' was a warrior's homecoming after war.

PENSIVE HEAD

After Wyndham Lewis

What is it about that Thirties palette?
Those browns, a decade-long autumn endlessly
taking leave of the branch: stoic farewells
on steam-swamped platforms, pensive heads
opaque through café windows; ducking down
to order soup through hatches, fingers like
rheumatic sausages prop sallow faces
bent over the tea cup of thwarted lives.
As if the brush knew what was coming,
as if it hunkers down in the spectrum's
trench: a reflex wrapped in khaki, nurtured
in mud and want. Of eyes that have witnessed
too much; that have seen the peacock's head
held under Brown Windsor, shot off above
the parapet of, say, ochre. At the quayside
dirty hankies wave goodbye to the red
neckerchiefs bound for Aragon, stand back
to let the tanks pass, wave through the ranks
of goose-stepping shirts; yes, those shirts.

MIDSUMMER

As though nothing happens
our hemisphere shoulders the sun,

the hill asleep on its trove of peat,
the sea is soaked in light.

In the days before Johnsmas
we bear fuel to the *sgùrr,*

our own brief blaze stoked
in its hours and seasons

by the darkness and the light.

MIDWINTER

Sun's pale wick
slants a glim
into the cairn's
stone gut
to glean
lost moment
from its nameless
priest-king,
is slaked
by the hill-line
black
over
Hoy,
skimps
a last
from
the year's
yielding
and
drops;
drops
below
world's
end
time's
end,
shifts
then
slow
to
the
onset.

STORM PETREL

Mousa, Shetland

Come back in Summer,
be here at nightfall,
put your ear to the
broch and listen as
the twittering mis-
fires of a thousand
tiny engines ig-
nite the wall with tales
of the ocean and
a life on the wing
flitting home to its
solitary egg.
In eight weeks they're gone:
birds of bad omen,
souls of lost sailors,
Mother Carey's Chicken.
Come, put your ear to
the broch and listen.

SUMBURGH, 1952

I

Advertisement

Good ones acquire the mettle for confinement
and the solitude of the wild shore. He will be
a handyman to a high standard and, through
study of the sea, he'll come to grasp its power.

The man of parts with a knack for engines,
at stations with radar or radio beacons
he'll have a flair for telecommunications.
A useful cook and good companion, he

won't make a fortune but will be at peace
with himself and the world. Main chores
are long hours in the watches of the night.
Not for everyone, this keeping of the light.

II

The Inspectors

Drop by here once a year,
so, everything is polished
and everyone well-dressed.
Spick-and-span is normal
– no more than our duty –
and we've enough men
to keep things gleaming.
Come when you want,
inspect what you will
fuss over this and that,
your visit holds no fear
for the likes of us.

III

The Lightkeeper's Daughter

We climb the stone wall
and edge down the slope
to watch puffins for hours,

snuggling into the cliff's nook,
me in Dad's coat out of the wind,
drinking tea from his thermos.

The way they flutter in to land,
like black and orange confetti,
is my door into summer.

Once, when we look down,
there's a huge shark cruising
at the foot of the bluff.

I remember thinking to myself
it's the biggest thing I've ever seen.
Daddy laughs and pulls me close.

IV

The Lightkeeper's Wife

There's always a good breeze up here to dry the washing out
and stuff to do with the hens or the vegetable patch.

Both bairns were born up at the Head, so it is all they've known,
they love this posting, play round about the light and pet the goat.

And the local folk look up to Bob, like he was the minister,
doctor or a teacher. We'll be sorry when the time comes.

BRIGHT COAST

For Bryan Angus

i.

this is understood:
drawn line of horizon
stretched across a bay
the gods died making,
morning's urgent grave
upon the gable end
and hands above
a woodblock, trimming
the void to light
as another day
answers for itself

ii.

art school of the brae
and cherryburn wren;
this valley thick with corn
and morning's ink of light;
return to me a childhood
type-high to the now
of a silver shilling;
gift me the sea's slow prism
and the lumen hours
of a northern shore
always at my shoulder,
always prone to rain

iii.

how it alters colour, how it
makes and unmakes shadow;
how it comes ready-made
by morning to the folded cliffs,
drawing at the core of it all,
as the winter sun's candela
scorps the six-hour day
from the hollow of my palm,
thumb along the blade,
resurfacing the light:
everything feeds into this

iv.

idiom of line and light,
the moon overprints
itself upon the block
of night
down
hillside
to the shore's rake;
drops Fresnel
onto slate roof
and dormer;
ghosts
among the lanes
of the sleeping town;
silversmiths
form into
well-wrought
dreams
of home
and the full-house
of this dark
ocean

v.

not simply the eye
alive to now
but a mind awake
to time and
the composite days
of this sickle strand,
its clarity of air,
patinas of slate
and sharply angled light,
askance upon
the boxwood:
these marks we make,
centre to edge,
block on the sandbag
aligned to the Pole.

THE TRAINING FOR LONELINESS

Until it was you, my son,
your father's best work
was that night in Manhattan,
alone in a mid-town hotel
but for the barman
from Roscommon
explaining to me
the finer points of hurling,
while I waited for the hour
to come and go when
we'd meet for that drink,
look one another in the eye,
and head our separate ways.

No sane woman would cross
the pond to drink to an also-ran,
so, I knew she wouldn't show
but the point was that I *had*
and there began my draft of you.
As the moment passed, I swear
That's Life lit up the jukebox
right on cue, as if it knew
a fool's errand was over.

Fíonn asked why I was laughing
as I drained my glass of *Powers*.
When I told him, he poured me
another and we got to talking,
as fellers sometimes do,
about loneliness and home
and the Great American Songbook
of lost love that crops up
at a time like this: your father,
as a younger man, trying to write
the poem that will become you
and is you and will go on
when this song is well-sung.

ACKNOWLEDGEMENTS:

Acknowledgements are due to the following publications, anthologies and online journals in which some of these poems, or versions of them, first appeared: *About Larkin, Acumen, Agenda, And Other Poems, The Attic Sessions #14, Bare Fiction, BBC website, Blackbox Manifold, Book 2.0, The Black Light Engine Room, Butcher's Dog, Cake, Dreamcatcher, Eborakon, Elbow Room, The Fat Damsel, The Frogmore Papers, The Galway Review, Haverthorn, Ink, Sweat & Tears, Iota, Letters To Barnacle, Lighthouse, Long Poem Magazine, Magma, The Moth, Muse, Northwords Now, Obsessed With Pipework, Orbis, Poetry Ireland Review, Poetry Salzburg, PORT, Prole, The Reader, Route 57, Scottish Poetry Library website, Smiths Knoll, Stand, STRIX. Under The Hedge* and *Under The Radar.* Also, *'The Naked Irish: Portrait of a Nation Beyond the Clichés', 'Pale Fire': The Frogmore Press Anthology of the Moon 2019, 'The Ecchoing Green': poems inspired by William Blake 2015 anthology, Vanguard Editions #1 Poetry Anthology 2014, Orkney Writers' Anthology 2017, 'Days Begin…' Poetry Wivenhoe Anthology, The Telltale Press Truth Anthology 2018, Hands & Wings Anthology 2015* and the Emma Press *Dance, Fatherhood* and *Love* anthologies. *The Waiting Hillside* won the inaugural Straid Poetry Award. 'Digitalis' won the Poetry Wivenhoe Competition 2011. 'Mrs. Mounter' won the 2012 Mirehouse Poetry Competition.

Thanks to my publishers John Lucas, Wolfgang Görtschacher, Alex MacMillan, Hilda Sheehan. p.a. morbid and Mark Davidson.

Author picture credit: Michael Macari / StAnza

Cover artwork credit: Bryan Angus

Martin Malone lives in north-east Scotland. He has published three poetry collections: *The Waiting Hillside* (Templar, 2011), *Cur* (Shoestring, 2015), *The Unreturning* (Shoestring, 2019) and four chapbooks: *17* Landscapes (Bluegate Books), *Prodigals* (The Black Light Engine Room), *Mr. Willett's Summertime* (Poetry Salzburg) and *Shetland Lyrics* (Hedgehog Poetry). He is an Associate Teaching Fellow in Creative Writing at Aberdeen University. For five years between 2013 and 2017, he was editor of *The Interpreter's House* journal.

Selected from his three collections and various pamphlet publications, *Larksong Static* offers a first synopsis of Martin Malone's work so far. From his resounding alliances of memory and geography in *The Waiting Hillside*, through the complicated emotional landscape and fine-art sensibilities of *Cur*, to the brilliantly achieved cultural memory work of his Great War sequence, *The Unreturning*, this selection captures a poet staking serious claim for his significance to the contemporary scene.